CATS

A COLLECTION OF
HEARTWARMING FURRY-TALES

volume 1

KATHRYN JANE

CATS: A Collection of Heartwarming Furry-Tales, Volume 1

By: Kathryn Jane

Cover by The Killion Group

Cover photo: Nano, by Shelly Roche

ISBN: 978-0-9949209-7-3

Also by Kathryn Jane

CATS Volume 2

INTREPID WOMEN SERIES
Book 1 – Do Not Tell Me No
Book 2 – Touch Me
Book 3 – Daring To Love
Book 4 – Voices
Book 5 – Lies
Book 6 – All She Wanted
Book 7 – Dance With Me
Book 8 – untitled (Spring, 2017)

CONTENTS

ACKNOWLEDGMENTS

Without the Killion Group designing my covers, Demon for Details doing a fabulous job of editing, Judicious Revisions proofreading and both Lucy j Charles and Barb lending their talents as critiquers, this book wouldn't look or sound anything like it does today.
Ladies, I thank you all profusely!

I would also like to humbly thank the board of TinyKittens for graciously allowing me to use the names Quark, Bobbi, Sisko, Toothless, Mila and Sloaney, as well as references to the Happy Forest in these fictional stories which are purely the product of my imagination.

DEDICATION

Volume 1 of CATS, is dedicated to
TinyKittens.com.
To the volunteers who keep the feral colonies and
TinyKittens HQ so well looked after.
To the chatters and lurkers who follow the progress of
each new kitten or feral project.
To those who believe ferals are just as worthy of love, care
and attention as all other cats.
To those who support TinyKittens through donations, or
by spreading the word about spaying and neutering, and
the value of community cats.
And finally, to Shelly Roche, because she brought the
world together to make a difference.
Rescuing locally, educating globally.

CATS–the series, is dedicated to
Bear and Wolfe,
a one of a kind pair of cats who were there for the first
book I ever wrote, and nearly every one since.
My boys, this series is for you.

.

1

PRINCESS

STRANGE new scents bombarded Princess while she peered out from under the gnarled stump where she'd taken shelter in the night. She blinked. It hadn't been a nightmare. She really *had* been yanked from her bed, stuffed in a box, and taken for a ride in the car.

Then tossed out alongside a highway.

The deafening noise of trucks and cars, and the box shifting with the wind of each passing vehicle, had been real. As had the blinding flashes of light when she finally ripped her way out of the prison they left her in. Claws on fire and gums bleeding, she fled blindly toward the darkness at the side of the road, racing—as though guided by an invisible hand—to this tiny sanctuary where she hid, panting, heart pounding, and petrified. Hours of silence and terror had been punctuated by the sounds of other creatures not far away.

In daylight, things were only slightly less frightening, and a shiver ran through her while she tried to make sense of what she saw. This place wasn't like anything she'd ever seen before. It was the outdoors, where she'd never been allowed to go, but it was different from her yard. The ground felt very curious compared to the miles of grass she remembered tickling her toes on the day she sneaked outside to visit with a handsome cat singing the song of her people.

He asked her to dance and she'd been flattered. Batted her eyelashes and never thought about how the dancing might make her feel. She had no mother to explain there would be a price for a day's freedom. But she'd been driven. Couldn't help herself, and now her humans hated her.

They hadn't put it in words, but there had been sharp looks, and after what they did last night, she could assume nothing else.

Princess shuddered, and shook off the sadness. She had things to do, although she wasn't sure what. And how could that be? How did she know to follow the scents to this place she now timidly surveyed?

Drawn by the irresistible presence of water, she carefully approached the wide silver dish, and wasted little time sniffing and tasting before crouching low to lap with vigor—to fill the emptiness in her belly.

Catching a faint whiff of food, she tossed caution aside to nose through a vast array of scattered dishes, but they were all empty save for a bit of crusting at the edge of one. She made short work of the miniscule offering before something else caught her attention.

Over by the trunk of a wide tree. Wasn't that a ratty toy like the one she had at home? *Oh, dear, how will I ever find my way home to my toys, soft bed, and food dishes? What am I to do?*

A bug skittered across her path, and without thought, she pounced on it. Crunched hungrily. And a vile taste filled her mouth. She shook her head, pawed at her mouth and drool dripped until the bitterness eased.

Best you don't try another of those. They're not meant for eating.

What? Who? She quickly swiveled around, trying to find the source of the voice, but saw no one. She backed toward the safety of her hollow. Or that's what she *thought* she was doing, but miscalculation had her hopping forward when her bottom made contact with something hard. She spun. It was the heavy tunnel thing she'd seen earlier, and inside, another muddy toy.

She slinked toward it for a sniff. It smelled like the earth. And other cats. That couldn't be a good thing. She backed out then, taking one careful step at a time, and rechecked the dishes for food.

They come later. You'll have to wait unless you fancy yourself a hunter.

She stayed very still, hoping to see movement from the owner of the voice, then gave up and asked, *Where are you?*

Close by.

There will be food later?

Yes. When the ladies come. It's quite wonderful. But you'll have to meet the others, and learn about the proper order of things first. There are rules.

Princess didn't mind rules. She'd already learned not to scratch the furniture, and to only get on the kitchen counter when no one was at home. But now she wasn't there, and the kids would miss her. Who would help them eat breakfast?

Princess quite liked the little circle things, especially when they were in the bottom of the bowl and soft from the milk.

The mother person always said she wasn't to have milk because it made her poo runny, but Princess loved the sweet taste, and the way the kids giggled when she ate from their bowls.

Her tummy growled, and she hunkered down to rest the noisiness on cold dirt. She'd had nothing to eat since dinner last night. And mornings at home always meant food from the can. *Oh, dear.* She slumped forward and rested her chin on her toes. Perhaps she could go home now.

She closed her eyes, then opened them quickly, hoping she'd find herself on the tiny pink bed that looked just like the one the little girl slept in. But she was still outdoors.

If you're hungry, you must do something about it.

I'm afraid I don't know how. She hesitated only a moment. *Could you help me?* She remembered her manners, *Please?*

A tiny cat the color of earth and leaves and bits of charred wood, sat up across the clearing from Princess. Good heavens, she must have been there the whole time, blending in perfectly with her surroundings.

She stretched, and strolled toward Princess, then sat again when she was very close. *You're quite wide. Some are clumsy with the weight of many kittens in their belly. Are you?*

I have eaten no kittens!

Good grief. The tiny cat yawned again. *How old are you?*

I'm not exactly sure, but the children had a party for my six-month birthday around the time they brought a tree indoors. One I was not allowed to climb, but I kept forgetting, because it had toys hanging from the branches. And many bright colors on a string, but the colors were very hot when I tried to catch them. And after a while, the tree was taken away. It was very cold outside back then, much colder than now—except for last night. I've never slept outdoors before.

Ah, well. You'd best come with me, and we'll get you and yours something to eat.

Princess followed the dainty cat, all the while feeling rather like an overstuffed pillow.

Excuse me, what is your name?

Her new friend glanced over her shoulder. *I'm Sisko. What do they call you?*

Princess.

Well, Princess, just like at the house where you lived, there are rules here, and they can be hard to learn but I'm here to help you. Do you see the tips of my ears? How one is flat? It means the people made it so I don't have to raise kittens anymore, which means I have

4

*time to spare. I could take you on and teach you the ways of the
colony to make sure you do okay here, but we'll see what the day
brings.*

Was she to live outdoors, then? Without a house? No
window ledges to lie on and watch the rain? No soft beds
to snuggle into? Oh, but this would take some getting used
to.

Princess followed her new friend. Ducked below
some branches, climbed over others. It was hard work to
keep her tummy from scraping. When she huffed a bit
while scrambling over a slippery green tree lying on the
ground, Sisko shushed her.

Princess tucked behind Sisko, where she was
crouched at the edge of a small, grassy area—not grass like
at home, but long and waving in the wind. Hadn't Sisko
promised her food? *Why are we sitting here?*

*I'm hunting. You'll need to stay absolutely still and watch what
I do.*

Okay. But how could her new friend really be hunting
if she wasn't even moving? Princess was confused, and too
tired to care. Her eyelids drooped.

Did you see that?

She startled. *What?*

The movement under the grass out there?

She fought to get her eyes open and look at the place
Sisko was staring at. Sure enough, there was the tiniest of
movements.

There's a creature under there. Stay here, and watch what I do.

Sisko moved one foot, then another. Stayed frozen in
place for a moment, then moved again and ever so slowly
continued the pattern until she reached the place where the
creature had been. Princess stifled a yawn.

Sisko's tail twitched, then she leapt through the air
and pounced and, oh, my goodness, she came bounding
back across the field with something in her mouth.

Things blurred a bit then for Princess, as her friend
taught her the rituals of giving the prey chances to escape,

then finally making a meal of it. Once finished, Princess felt somewhat uncomfortable, but her tummy no longer hurt, and she just couldn't stay awake.

Slip back under the stump and take a nap. I'll stand guard.

Princess needed no extra urging, and fell into such a deep sleep, that when she eventually woke up she was disoriented.

Was she at home? No, there was still that damp, earthy smell. She crawled out and found Sisko there, as she'd promised, but the forest had changed. She was surrounded by movement and great excitement filled the air. *What is it? What's going on?*

It's nearly time.

Caw! Caw!

Princess dove back into her hidey-hole. Peeked out. *What was that?*

Nothing bad, just Jake. He's a crow. He waits in a tree by the highway and signals when they're coming.

Who?

The nice ladies who bring the food.

That perked Princess up. And she boldly stepped into the open to sit beside Sisko.

There were cats everywhere she looked. Orange ones, black ones, gray ones, some wearing many colors like Sisko, but none white with orange patches like Princess and the mom she barely remembered.

A few stared at her, but most didn't even notice she was there before they all suddenly scooted down a narrow pathway. *Where are they going?*

To meet the ladies.

The food ladies?

Yes.

Oh, let's go too! I'm very hungry again.

You must wait. There is an order, and because you are new, you'll eat after everyone else is finished. We'll stay here until it's your turn.

But what if they eat it all?

The ladies know about hidden cats, the ones who don't come out until later to eat.

Do I have to hide, then?

No, I want them to see you so they might help you. Take you to the place.

The place?

Where scary but magical things happen, and there is always food, and you can see the outside but can't touch it.

What if I don't like the place?

If you hate it there, once the kittens are old enough, they'll bring you back here.

What kittens?

Shh. They're coming.

Princess craned her neck to see past Sisko, and watch the excitement. Oh, my, there were even more cats now, and many ran through the forest, keeping pace with the lady. Her arms were wrapped around a huge sack and bags hung from her shoulder.

"You guys are going to trip me one of these days." She laughed and her glance swung past Princess. Stopped and tracked back.

"Well, we have a new member, I see. Hello, sweet kitten. Aren't you pretty?"

The dozen or more cats meowing at the lady's feet dragged her attention back to the job at hand, and she busily filled dishes with dry food. The smell, the sound of happy crunching had Princess's tummy growling so loudly in protest she longed to push past Sisko and go to the food, but couldn't. Not after her new friend's unwavering kindness. Instead she mimicked Sisko's position, complete with her front toes folded under, and waited.

It seemed to take an awfully long time, but she knew it truly wasn't. Not long like when the kids went to school and she was alone in the house. Oh, my, this was nothing like the house where she lived—or had until last night when the mother came to get her from where she was sleeping on the little girl's bed. Said they had no room.

7

Only wanted one cat. They'd get a male next time, so kittens would be someone else's problem. Princess hadn't understood what she meant.

She's coming.

Princess looked up to find the lady very close to them. She had a soothing voice, and kept talking quietly while offering a dish filled with food. Sisko backed away. *Go, eat, and let her pet you. She'll take care of you.* Sisko skittered to a food container farther from the lady.

"You're very pretty, and I bet you're hungry." The lady knelt, put the dish on the ground and Princess simply couldn't resist. She took one step, another, and was suddenly so lost in the smell, the taste, she completely forgot her manners. Gobbled without looking up.

When the dish was nearly empty, she realized the lady was stroking her, and talking into one of those sorta square flat things like the people at her house did. "She's big like a pumpkin, and definitely not feral. Hang on, I'll send you a video." She held the square thing toward Princess for a minute, then put it back to her ear and laughed.

"I'll figure something out and meet you there." She ran her hand down Princess's back. "This, my friend, is your lucky day. And I'm about to do something I shouldn't do, but I'm betting you'll be good with it."

So happy with a full tummy, Princess didn't even squirm when the lady lifted her into one of the big bags she'd been carrying when she arrived. When the top was folded over and she couldn't see, there was a moment of fear—because of the box the night before—but Sisko's voice soothed her.

She's kind, Princess, and she's taking you to a special place, where you'll never have a worry again. After the kittens are weaned, you'll get a wonderful forever home with people you can trust.

Okay. She let herself relax and enjoy the warmth she could feel coming from where she was held close against the lady.

"I'll be back in about a half hour to finish up," the

lady told the gathered cats as she marched past them. "And as for you, pretty girl, I'm betting the last car ride you were on ended badly, but this time, it will be much better."

Happy life, Princess!

Thank you for helping me, Sisko!

When they were inside the car, the lady let Princess peek out of the bag, and rubbed her ears until purring started.

"Your babies will be born in a warm, safe place, and after they've gone off to homes of their own, you'll be spayed and you'll never have to worry about kittens again. Then you'll get a fabulous home, too."

She liked the sound of a fabulous new home, but why did everyone keep talking about kittens?

***

PRINCESS recognized the scent that came with a house. The way people smells were embedded in the floors and walls, and the lights made the air different. There were many other things, too, stuff she'd never bothered to think about until she was in the forest for the first time.

She could also smell cats. Lots of cats.

A second lady had brought a crate from the house to the car, and Princess went inside it to get the toona she could smell. She didn't mind when the door closed to keep her trapped, and she'd almost finished the plate of goodness by the time she was lowered to the floor inside the house. Now she could do nothing but wait to find out what would happen next.

"Hey, pretty girl, this is going to be a very good day for you, so just hang in there while I gather some things. Be right back." The house lady sounded very nice, but Princess didn't care for being left in the crate, and she pushed at the door with her nose, but it didn't budge. She dug the blankets away from the front, then used her sore claws to pull at the door but it stayed firmly fastened.

"Meoooooow!"

"Goodness," said the forest lady as she came back through the doorway. "You have quite the voice."

"Meooooooooow!"

She laughed. "I get it. You want out. Just give me a sec." She scooted out of sight, then a door slammed somewhere in the house.

"She's not happy about being locked up."

"Well," said the house lady, "I guess we'd better let her out, then." She crouched in front of the cage. "Welcome to Rescue HQ, pretty one."

When she opened the cage, Princess scooted past her, only to stop in the middle of the room, uncertain where to go, or what to do next.

"How about another snack?" said forest lady, and the sound of the top coming off a can had Princess's full attention. She'd love more of the toona.

A dish was set in front of her. Her nose twitched. Not toona, but it smelled delicious, so she dug right in, and didn't mind having the ladies sit on the floor beside her.

"Poor girl looks ready to burst." A gentle hand stroked down her back.

"Probably due any minute." Another hand slipped under her belly. "After your call, I tried to get us an ultrasound appointment, but they're doing an emergency surgery right now, and have a stack of people waiting. The soonest I could get was tomorrow at four."

"Let's hope she doesn't have them in the night. I guess it would save the expense of the ultrasound, though."

"True, but she looks really young, still a kitten herself, and it's much better to know how many babies are in there, just in case she has trouble delivering. It will also give us a better idea how far along she is, whether there's six or seven half-cooked, or three ready to pop out any minute."

Princess continued licking the plate while wondering what the ladies were talking about, and once there wasn't a morsel left, she quickly washed her face, then went exploring. She had a yen for small spaces lately, and longed for a soft spot to sleep.

She'd found the perfect place in the bottom of a closet at home just a few days ago, but now she didn't have an "at home." She shook off the sadness threatening to overwhelm her, threw herself into searching, and scored right away.

It was kind of like the kitchen cupboard the mother person wouldn't let her play in, but with no pots and things. Instead, the floor of this one was lined with fluffy blankets.

She dug and rooted around until she'd made it just right, kneaded a bit, then snuggled in for a nap. But couldn't fall asleep.

Maybe there was a better place. She prowled, found another cabinet thing with more cushy blankets and again, after some rearranging, tried to settle in for a sleep, but the thought of the first bed niggled at her. Maybe it *had* been softer.

Or maybe there was an even better bed she hadn't seen yet. She combed the room this time. Every corner, nook, and cranny. Found quite a few places she could make a bed of, but in the end, went back to the first one, where she'd almost fallen asleep when the ladies started talking.

"Definitely nesting, and she's huge."

"Yeah, no way I'm leaving this catermelon alone tonight," said the house lady.

Princess poked her head out to watch them set up a bed on skinny legs, then top it with a pillow, and a sleeping bag. Princess loved sleeping bags. So soft and warm and you could hide inside them to play or nap.

She yawned. Time for that nap now.

But she must have eaten too much. Her tummy hurt,

and she kept moving around to find a better position. For hours she went from one bed to the next, digging at the blankets, shoving them aside, piling them up, she even tried wedging herself into a small space behind one of the cabinets, but that didn't work, either. And then the pain grew unbearable, and the lady was there talking to her, telling her everything would be okay.

But it wasn't, because something was wrong, very, very wrong, and she needed to be rid of whatever it was crawling around inside of her. She went to the box and had a poop, but didn't feel any better, so she stretched out on the cool floor for a while, dozed off and on until a pain ripped through her belly and went all the way to her toes. She shot to her feet and headed back to the first bed.

In the safety of the cabinet, she strained to work with the constant ache, and the house lady opened the doors to lean in and tell her over and over again what a good job she was doing.

Oh, the comfort coming from that voice, from the hand stroking gently over her head while time passed in a haze of agony.

There was a spot under her tail that seemed to need her attention and Princess tried numerous times, but couldn't reach around her massive belly to tend to the problem.

Then she had to push from inside. She strained and strained and suddenly there was a thing. A wet, wiggling bundle, and she desperately needed to take care of it. Anxious to get it free of the sack it was in, she somehow knew...

It was a kitten!

But terribly wet, and she had to get it dry. Quickly. She licked and licked, and it started making little squeaky sounds, then—

The torment started again, and something else was suddenly there, and she had to clean *it* up right away. Keep it away from her kitten. *Her* kitten. How crazy was that?

But the torturous stabbing through her insides hadn't gone away and now she understood. Another kitten was coming. She had to leave the first while she got the next one out. Strained. Nothing happened. The pain ate at her strength.

"What a good mama you are." The now familiar voice was kind, soothing. "I can help you a bit, okay?"

She watched the lady take the kitten and rub it with a towel until it started squeaking again, and then the lady put it back beside Princess. "Here you go, she's nice and dry and ready for milk bar."

Another massive pain sliced through Princess, and a second kitten came from inside her, and then everything blurred together. Pain, another kitten, clean…over and over it happened, and when she was getting too tired to go on, the lady gave her food, and helped cut cords and dry off babies until finally Princess was done. Finished. Exhausted and sore. And her insides kept cramping and cramping, even though she was finally empty.

This was why Sisko had gone on and on about kittens. For just a moment, Princess let her gaze rest on the little ones pulling on her nipples. Then she lowered her head and let sleep drag her away while the lady kept talking to someone who wasn't there.

"Final count is seven, every one of them ginger and white, just like mama. Three girls and four boys, all latched on."

2

SISKO, QUARK, AND MILA

BACK in the forest, Quark's velvety voice slipped into Sisko's mind.

Well done, my dear.

Princess? She glanced toward the special place where a single sunbeam lay warm on the earth beside Quark's marker.

Yes, you made an excellent decision.

I could see no point trying to make her comfortable here when she was clearly not one of us, and better suited to a life with humans. Poor little thing didn't even know she was about to have kittens.

Seven. And all delivered safely.

A curious warmth stole through Sisko. *Wonderful.*

Mila sat down beside her. *Your voice sounded very far away. Were you talking to me?*

No, to Quark.

Mila ducked her head in respect for the dead, and whispered, *Can you see her?*

Of course not.

Then how?

When she visits and I hear her voice, there's always a tiny patch of sunlight on her resting place. I just imagine her curled up there enjoying the sun.

Where is she when she's not visiting here?

In a very special place, Mila. Quark's voice was as warm as the sunbeam. *With friends and family who've gone before me.*

Mila ducked her head again in deference. *Is it the place where Sisko and I were taken? With the magic portal to the outside? The one we couldn't pass through, but where we were safe from the predators?*

No, Mila. It is like that in a way, because there are no threats to our safety, or rain, or snow, and the food dishes are always full. But this other place is across a special rainbow bridge, in a forest where clean, fresh water bubbles up from the ground, food is plentiful, and there are lots cozy beds on soft furniture, in fine straw, and even high up in the trees—like nests for eagles. It is so pretty to look down from there.

Mila suddenly jumped to her feet. *It sounds wonderful! May I go there with you?*

No, my dear. You have work to do yet.

Work? I don't understand.

You must help the others.

How? What should I do?

I don't know what your calling is, my dear. That's something you must figure out for yourself.

What was yours? What did you have to do?

While I was a happy forest cat, it was my duty to encourage the ladies. To welcome them every day, and show them what a wonderful family we were, and that we are well worth their efforts. It's why I allowed them to befriend me, greeted them each and every day, and showed how much we appreciate their care, and what they do for all of us.

Mila was confused. *But like everyone else, you were taken away for the operation, and the end of your ear was cut off…*

And came back a better cat for their kindness. I was very proud to show the others my tipped ear, my symbol. Grateful to no longer need to scramble to provide for kittens in the cold and wet, protect them from predators, and watch them die no matter how hard I tried to care for them.

Mila and Sisko were both nodding. *Terribly*

disheartening to lose them in spite of our dedication.

You must share your experience with your sisters, your daughters, the youngsters. Show them how proud you are of your tipped ear, and give them the confidence they need to go into the traps.

Mila got it. *Like when Sisko helped Amber last week!*

Yes, that's it. Amber will be safe while she has her kittens, and won't have to fear for them. And when they're old enough to get by without her, the ladies will bring her back here, and she'll have her symbol. Become an ambassador like both of you.

Mila shook her head. But I don't actually live with this colony, I only visit now and again, so I'm not often around when the ladies come.

You encounter many cats where you live. You can help by sending them here so they get fixed up with their own ear tip.

I can do that. She glanced around, then whispered, *Why did you come here today?*

To thank Sisko for looking after Princess. I'm going back to my other happy place now, though, as I'm due for a nap. Be well, Sisko and Mila. I trust you'll handle the next event without the need for my return.

The tiny sunbeam faded and, as always, Sisko felt an odd pressure in her heart, because she always worried whether this might be the last time the guardian queen came to visit. *Goodbye, Quark, and thank you for watching over us.*

Mila crept over to the now-dark area near the marker. Sniffed the air, then turned to *Sisko. Her scent is here, yet I couldn't see her.*

It's always that way with the spirit cats.

There are others?

Of course. We're never truly alone.

Mila thought about it. *Sisko?*

Hmm? Her friend sounded sleepy.

My kittens. The ones who didn't get to grow up. Are they in that happy place where Quark lives?

Yes, Mila.

She curled up alongside her friend. *I lost so many over*

the years, it must be very crowded there.

Quark says not. There are endless acres for them.

I wonder if my kittens know each other there.

When I asked Quark about my last son, Toothless, she said he was with his brothers and sisters who'd gone before him.

That's lovely, very lovely. I shall sleep now, and dream of my kittens in a happy place, too.

3

CHARCOAL

AFTER a long nap on a soft bed made of something like clouds, Quark returned to the forest to bask in the sun puddle near her marker. She liked visiting her family, especially on days like today, when the sun was warm and bellies were full.

A pair of tabbies napped close by—well, actually, one wasn't sleeping. Instead, he kept watch while his brother slept peacefully beside him.

Wheezy snores, and the flutter of birds flitting among the branches were the only sounds to be heard.

Quark tipped her head up to take in the lingering odor of canned food, the dampness of earth, and something else with a sharp edge to it.

She scanned, finally caught movement at the far side of the feeding ground, and kept watch while a family of skunks foraged for scraps—bits of kibble missed by the felines.

Their visit meant there would be no waste, which was good, but it also meant there would be nothing left for someone she knew would arrive shortly, and would be the neediest of all.

Quark positioned herself beside the only dish with

food still in it. The ladies never left much behind, for fear of attracting predators. When the skunks approached, she huffed a breath toward the mama—even though Quark was invisible, she was able to move air. Pleased to see the pointy black nose come up, she huffed a second time, and a funny sound rumbled in the mama's chest before she spun and headed back the way she came. Her kits scurried in her wake with tiny black and white tails waving like flags.

As if on cue, movement to the right caught Quark's eye.

A grubby-looking tuxie, nothing but bones, hollows, and matted black fur came into view. Hobbled from one empty dish to the next while struggling to keep a front leg from touching the ground.

She paused as though too tired to go on, but just when Quark was about to nudge her, she mustered the strength to continue. Unable to watch her fruitlessly circling in the wrong direction, Quark slipped alongside to gently guide her by creating a bit of resistance. But the starving creature pushed back, refusing to be put off course, so Quark went to plan B. Stood over the full dish, and blew a soft breath across the food.

The tuxie lifted her head, sniffed the air, and, suddenly appearing stronger, she made a three-legged beeline to the food, not stopping until she was wolfing down kibble.

Quark sat back, pleased with the outcome, but puzzling over how to deal with this newcomer. Would she be able to outrun a predator? Not likely, but was it because she was on three legs, or because she was starving? Would she be safe enough here at the colony for her leg to heal? Possibly, and a steady supply of food would help.

Luckily, the ladies had left just enough for this tiny tuxie to get a good meal into her tonight. Then Quark would reassess.

Up until now, she'd never used her position to call

the ladies back to the feeding station after they'd left for the day, but there was a first time for everything. All Quark would have to do was ask Bobbi to help.

Before she ran out of lives, Bobbi had been with the people for a few years, and understood them, so she'd be able to stir one of the ladies up enough to bring them here. But Quark wouldn't use that resource unless absolutely necessary. And there was work to be done first.

Hello. Quark kept her internal voice at a low and comforting hum, like she used to do with her kittens long ago. The tuxie stilled.

My name is Quark, and I'm here to help you.

The newcomer's dirt-crusted pink and white nose twitched, and she moved her golden eyes, as though searching for the source of the voice.

Now you've had a meal, I'd like to talk with you.

Quark is an unusual name. Are you a guardian?

Yes. What is your name?

They call me Charcoal.

You have people?

Not anymore. They got a new baby and were afraid I'd smother it, so I had to live outside.

Good grief. Why would anyone have such a crazy thought?

What does it matter? She attempted to wash her face, but couldn't hold her weight on the injured leg, and finally gave up.

How long have you been on your own?

A while. It was fun at first, stalking prey through the long grass, and lying in the sun. But then I learned not all dogs were like the one I used to live with.

You were chased.

Worse, I was caught. You see, when I realized the dog wasn't friendly and spun to get away, he managed to grab me by the leg. Shook me like a stuffed toy. It was awful, but then it was better, because when he suddenly dropped me and ran off with his tail between his legs, I met Rena, a guardian angel like you. She had no body, but her voice was lovely, and I could feel her kindness.

Did she stay with you?

For a while, until it was time for her to cross the bridge. She offered to take me along, but said I might not be ready like she was. She'd just been waiting for her family to not need her anymore. They'd recently gotten their smiles back by rescuing another kitten, so she was free to go.

Quark had heard of this kind of thing many times. Souls not willing to cross over until those who loved them were ready to live whole again.

Quark, on the other hand, was allowed to cross back and forth at will, because she had taken on guardianship of her colony.

Rena was worried about my ability to hunt because of my leg. She told me I was to come to this place, and I've been traveling for a very long time. I wasn't sure sometimes if I'd ever get here, but she made me promise to not give up.

Charcoal curled into a ball and sighed. *And it was a very hard promise to keep. But I didn't let her down. I made it, which means it's okay to die now.* Her voice was soft, sleepy.

What? That's crazy. Why give up now you're here?

I needed to prove I was better than the people who tossed me out like trash, and I've done it. I made it here on three legs, and I was determined not to die with an empty belly. I'm full now, and I know I am worthy of the place on the other side of the bridge.

And worthy of rescue. Wouldn't you like to have a real home? One where you're loved and respected? Where your life will matter?

Of course.

Then you shall have it. By this time tomorrow, you'll be in a warm, safe place—as long as you do as I say. Are you willing?

Charcoal struggled up to a sitting position. *I'd give you a head-bump right now if I could see you.*

Quark smiled in the special way that made her visible, and the tuxie didn't even seem surprised to suddenly see a large gray cat sitting beside her.

Charcoal leaned over and turned so she could touch the guardian's forehead with her own, and she sighed. *Thank you.*

You need sleep now. Come with me. Quark led her a few steps to where sunshine warmed the ground in front of a wooden cross. *I will watch over you.*

Charcoal curled into a tiny ball, with only her injured leg sticking out, and drifted into a dreamless sleep, one she awoke from feeling somewhat refreshed, and warm from the sunbeam still touching her.

She glanced around at the big trees and underbrush. And dark shadows. Her heart pounded faster and faster against her ribs, and the throbbing in her foot increased. She was out in the open, exposed. Suddenly worried about what might have woken her up, she slinked, ever so slowly, toward the nearest tree. Even though she doubted her ability to climb, just the giant's presence, and the slightly pungent odor of the rough bark, helped to ease her fear.

With the tree at her back, she carefully scanned the area for movement, sniffed the air for the telltale smell of a predator, and swiveled her ears to catch every sound. Nothing. She was alone.

No, you're not, Charcoal. I'll be by your side until you leave here. The sound of Quark's voice was calming.

Thank you. I feel very blessed to have another angel guarding me. I know not everyone is as lucky.

You have three lives left, my friend, and will have a great impact in all of them. It is my job to help you get there.

Charcoal wasn't surprised by what Quark told her. Rena, the other angel, had said something similar, about there being a purpose for her survival. And somewhere deep inside, Charcoal knew this to be true. She could only wonder what she'd been assigned to do.

You are going to make a difference in the world one day, but your journey has many twists and turns yet. What I do know for sure is in the end you will be greatly loved.

Charcoal had felt love once, when she was a tiny kitten at a pet store. There was a little girl who visited her several times, and always placed her hand against the wires of the cage. Something about the child's scent had felt familiar, and Charcoal couldn't help but be drawn to the small human. Had purred when a fingertip pressed through the opening to stroke her head. Made her feel safe in the cage filled with strange cats, all of them scared, in a place where a constant barrage of sounds echoed.

The memory was so clear in Charcoal's mind, it felt like she was back there.

"Please, Papa, could I just hold her?"

"I don't know, Melissa." He'd looked around the cramped room behind the cages.

"If she sits down there on the floor, it would be okay," said the sales clerk minding the door. Then a huge hand reached in to lift Charcoal out of the cage and place her in the child's lap. Fingers closed gently around the kitten as she was lifted to snuggle against a fluffy white sweater.

"You're so beautiful, and soft, and warm," said Melissa. The kitten's purring instantly altered to keep time with the child's fluttering heart until a strong beat took over, and Charcoal drifted off to sleep.

The child's second and third visits ended the same way. Then Charcoal was adopted, and never saw her sweet visitor again, but that taste of love was never forgotten.

Not that her adopters were bad, they just lost interest in her when she wasn't a kitten anymore, but it was okay, because there was still good food to eat, and Charcoal liked to snuggle with the dog at night when they were locked in the utility room together.

Life had been pretty darned good until the lady's belly grew, and there was talk of how they would need to keep the cat away from the baby, and then Charcoal had suddenly become an outdoor cat. She was still able to come in at night for a while, as long as she was waiting at the door when they brought the dog in.

But staying out was great fun, because stalking tiny creatures in the moonlight was something she'd only dreamed about before. Eventually, however, her food dish was left on the porch, along with the small, round bed she'd slept in since she came home from the pet store. And sometimes the dish had no food in it, and Charcoal's need to hunt had taken her miles and miles from home.

After she was injured and drew the attention of Rena, the guardian had guided her even farther away. Said she needed to go to a special place in the forest.

Yes, she thought, after the last weeks of struggle, love would be nice. She closed her eyes and dreamed of warm hands, and a human heart beating close to her own.

***

THE next afternoon, dozens of cats suddenly appeared in the clearing moments before Jake sounded the alarm.

Caw! Caw!

Charcoal jumped. *What the—?*

Quark chuckled. *It's just Jake announcing the arrival of today's food lady.*

Many of the cats streaked through the woods to wait at the roadside where the lady parked, while some positioned themselves on the pathway she'd walk once she left her car. Still others hung back, waiting around the outside edge of the feeding area.

Arms filled with bags, the lady came down the trail, waving a stick. *She doesn't like the spider webs,* Quark explained to Charcoal.

"You'll be tripping me soon," the lady told a giant ginger who'd crossed in front of her. "Pick a side, you silly thing, before I step on you." She laughed when he crossed her path again, but then she stopped and stared at Charcoal where she was hunkered down in the sunbeam beside Quark's grave marker.

"Hello," the voice softened even more. "Who are you, pretty one?"

Should I go to her? asked Charcoal.

25

No, she has things to do. Just wait here, and she'll come back.

"Are you hungry?" the lady asked. "I have some great food with me. Just let me get it dished out to this motley crew first, and then I'll bring you some, okay?"

Charcoal stayed where she was.

Soon, cats of every color, shape, and size were scarfing down kibble from the containers being set around the area. Then the top was pulled off a can, and several heads came up. The big ginger left his crunchies to wind around the lady's leg.

"This is a welcome gift for the newcomer," she said, but put some in a dish for him, too. "Yes, you're spoiled, aren't you?" She rubbed a hand down his back, then made her way over to where Charcoal waited.

"You don't seem to be afraid of me. Would you like some of this nice, mushy food?"

Charcoal struggled to sit up.

"Oh, you poor thing." She set the dish down, and watched Charcoal hobble over to eat. Then she did what Quark was hoping for. She pulled the magic thing from her pocket and talked into it.

"We've got an injured stray sitting in Quark's spot."

She nodded.

"Bone thin, not the least bit afraid of me, and the right front leg is a mess. Extremely swollen and oozing. Really needs a vet."

"Yep, I have a crate in my car, but I'm afraid to let this one out of my sight. I know it's not protocol, but I could pull off my hoodie and use it to get as far as the car."

She smiled. "Yeah, I'll call you back."

She stuck the square thing back into her pocket, then pulled the shirt over her head and messed with the strings. "There. The hood end is secure at least." She knelt in the dirt and leaned toward Charcoal, who was now licking the sides of the empty dish.

The lady slid a hand over the tuxie, and when

Charcoal didn't flinch, with the ease of much practice, she slipped the hoodie over the cat and scooped her up.

Charcoal's instant purr was music to Quark's ears.

Goodbye, Charcoal, be well, little one.

Thank you, Quark. I'll never forget your kindness.

Quark glanced around the clearing, and saw all the cats staring at the place where the sun touched the earth just below her marker. They knew. And that added to the glow in her heart.

***

WARM inside the hoodie, Charcoal suddenly realized how cold she'd been. That's when the shivering started, and pain shot through her. But she tried to ignore it, concentrating instead on the nice scent of the lady, and her singsong voice.

"Hang in there, sweetie, I know you must be in agony, but we're going to get you fixed up, and I promise you all the food you can eat. I guess you haven't been able to hunt since your leg must hurt terribly. No wonder your bones are poking out."

Food would be good. She'd only just had a little bit, and already could use a bunch more.

When they reached the car, she was carefully set inside a crate and taken to a place where the air was filled with the smell of fear and sickness, but soft voices soothed while gentle hands checked her injured leg.

"The good news is I don't think anything's broken; the bad news is the nasty infection in these puncture wounds. We'll get some good pain meds into her first, plus antibiotics, then we'll get this mess cleaned up and flushed out." The vet's fingertips rubbed her underside, then she was turned onto her back and there was more groping.

"More good news, she's already been spayed."

"Excellent. Someone at least cared enough to do that."

"Although she has no tattoo or micro-chip, there's still a chance she might just be lost," said the vet.

"Possible. But we'll foot her bills for now, get her healed up and fed."

"Poor little girl needs a name. How about Hope?"

"Perfect." Gentle fingertips ran over the top of her head. "You are now officially called Hope."

It was odd to be given another identity, but at the same time, it felt rather good…or was it the drugs they'd given her? No matter. She did have hope now, and she'd gladly answer to a new name, and leave poor, hopeless Charcoal behind.

The rest of her time at the vet's office went by in a blur. There'd been pain, but the vet lady and the others kept promising she'd feel better soon. And she did. Even the leg inside the big pink bandage didn't throb now.

But then she was back in the car and taken to another place for what was called intake. There'd been a lot of poking—things in her ears, which had felt pretty good, then something in her butt, which hadn't, but was removed when a funny beeping sounded.

"There, Miss Hope, the bad stuff's over," said a new lady, who seemed to be in charge.

"I wish we could give her a bath," said another.

"We'll just have to fake it." She ran the tap until steam was rising and Hope fully expected to be dipped into the sink. She was no stranger to baths. Her owners had bathed her a lot because they said she smelled funny.

A cloth was dipped in the hot water, wrung out, and then rubbed all over Hope, and it felt really, really good.

The lady laughed. "Just listen to her purr. I think maybe she was tired of being dirty."

Oh, yes, but it had been so hard to wash herself because of her swollen leg. It wouldn't support her when she leaned over, and she could only lie on one side, so her once luxurious coat was a matted mess.

The ladies worked on her for a very long time, finally

switching to dry towels. Which was when she managed to slide off the table and into a lap.

It had been a very long time since Hope felt this good, but she had no more energy for purring, and the food she'd eaten while they worked on her was making her very sleepy. Maybe she'd just close her eyes for a minute.

While she drifted in the lovely world between asleep and awake, the two ladies continued to talk in low voices.

"Poor little thing's exhausted."

"But at least her tummy's full, she's warm, and she's safe. I can't imagine how long it's been since she dared allow herself a real nap."

"Yeah. I'll just hang here with her and get the paperwork done before we move her. Let her rest for a while. She's had a big day."

"I hate that she has to stay in the shelter while she recovers."

"Better than where she's been for heaven knows how long. And with the foster homes full right now, there's no other option."

A huge sigh came from the lap lady. "I could take her home with me for a few days."

Charcoal slipped into a deeper sleep. Everything was going to be okay, just like the guardian angels promised, and one day she'd find out why she was saved.

4

SWIRL AND FANTA

AFTER lurking for a while at the edge of the place where the food came, the kitten had finally worked up the courage to sneak toward a dish when the lady's soft voice floated across the clearing—as though meant just for her.

"Come on, little one, you can do it. I won't hurt you, just ask your friends." Without looking directly at the hungry kitten, she slowly lifted her hand toward the group gathered. "See, they're not afraid of me, and you don't have to be, either."

The tiny kitten's tummy was so terribly empty, she threw caution to the wind and crept closer to the wonderful smell.

"Good girl. How very brave you are. But then all calicos are brave. I love the pretty pattern of ginger and black on your side, so I'm going to name you for that. From here on in, you are Swirl."

The kitten didn't care about names right now. She reached out a paw to touch the food in the bowl, then drew back and licked it clean. Suddenly finding herself purring and unable to stop, she stole a bit closer. Used her paw a few more times, and then leaned in to lick the food right out of the dish.

Fear was instantly shoved aside, and she gulped great mouthfuls without taking her gaze off the lady who was now sitting on a log holding up a square sort of thing. It was the soft smile on her face that held Swirl mesmerized even after she'd cleaned the bowl of every morsel.

"Look at how very brave you've been. Would you like some more?"

While Swirl licked her lips, a bold tabby rubbed against the lady's legs, and a ginger allowed the touch of her hand.

"I have more right here." She set another full dish on the ground, but not nearly as close to the kitten.

Swirl badly wanted the more the lady offered, but to approach a person? The word predator whispered in the back of her mind. Her mama had warned her over and over again, long before they'd left the nest in the barn. Beware, she'd said, of the human predator. They eat little kittens.

Why would this lady eat her when she was only *half* a meal compared to the other cats? Oh how terribly hungry she was. Until today she'd been sneaking in after the ladies went away and scarfing down the dry food left by the others, and drinking the clear, cool water in the big dishes. But this. This mushy food was wonderful. She licked her lips again, to savor the memory of what she'd just eaten.

"Come on, Swirl, show the others how brave you are."

But I'm not brave! I'm only hungry, and my mama has new kittens to feed. She said it was time for me and my brother to join the other cats. There had been many days and nights since then, and now Swirl was alone.

Not completely alone, little one. I'm still watching over you.

Swirl glanced around, which was silly. She'd never seen Quark. Only ever heard her voice, and occasionally felt her comforting touch.

Be brave, little one. The lady will never hurt you. Go and get the food she's offering.

Swirl swallowed hard. Took one step. Another.

"Look how brave you are, Miss Swirl."

She didn't feel brave. Her heart was pounding, her paws shaking as they touched the ground, and she wanted to turn tail and dash for the safety of her hidey-hole. The safe place she'd found halfway up an old dead tree, where she could wedge herself in and sleep without fear of coyotes and other predators.

"You're almost here. Just a couple more steps."

She stared at the human's eyes. Assessing, and seeing nothing frightening there, she continued carefully placing one tentative foot in front of the other. Standing still now, within reach of the food, could she take that final step?

She did, grabbed a bite and jumped back while she swallowed. Sneaked forward again, and continued repeating the process until the dish was empty and her belly was swelled fatter than it had ever been.

The lady talked to Swirl the whole time she ate, and there was something quite mesmerizing about that voice, the way it just slipped through the air without disturbing it.

She retreated to where she could keep an eye on the human, and give herself a good wash. Mmmm. It would be a long time before she forgot the amazing taste. And the feeling of not being even a little bit hungry.

"I'm quite late now, and I have to run, Miss Swirl. I'm very glad you came to eat today, and I hope you're here when I come back on Thursday. Someone else will be here to feed tomorrow, and you'll like her, too, so be brave again, and she'll make sure you get a special meal."

With that, she slowly rose from the log she'd been sitting on, gathered up her bags and things, and went down the trail toward the road.

When quiet settled over them, most of the cats trundled off to their favorite napping spots, and Swirl followed suit. It would take a very long time to recover from such a meal. She longed to curl up on the spot, but knew better, and made her way to the safe place before giving in to oblivion.

Days passed, and she bravely attended every feeding, gradually becoming accustomed to the ladies who brought the food. And she learned the value of order, would always wait her turn. She made some friends, too, when three other kittens were evicted from their nests because their mamas had new babies. She showed the three the ways of the forest as the angel Quark had taught her. And they played games with pinecones, and the toys the ladies brought.

Swirl barely fit in her safe place now, so she and the other youngsters took to sleeping in one of the barns not far away, behind a row of barrels. And that's where the trouble began.

She'd been asleep, snuggled in beside her best friend, Fanta, a bright ginger with a pretty white nose and toes. Because they'd played hard in the wee hours of the morning while the moon made everything nearly bright as day, they slept later than usual, and were still behind the barrels when the barn doors opened and the men came in.

Too late now to get to the safety of the rafters, Swirl and Fanta crouched low, waiting for the voices to go by, but they didn't. And then there was a machine so loud Swirl's head hurt from the noise, and unbidden, a growl rose from her throat. Fanta hissed. But their efforts went unheard, and then there was a horrendous scraping sound when the heavy, grain-filled barrel began to move.

Swirl and Fanta backed into the smallest of spaces left to hide in, and then the unthinkable happened. The barrel tipped up and away from them, then slammed back into place, only closer to the wall, so the edge landed on Fanta's foot, and she screamed.

The machine shut off.

"What?" shouted a man.

"I heard something. You got a flashlight in that thing?"

"Sure. Wait a sec."

There were a couple of clangy noises Swirl recognized as a man climbing down off a tractor, then many footsteps on the concrete floor.

A bright light shone behind the barrels. "Shit. Couple of cats trapped back here."

Swirl positioned herself in front of Fanta, and she hissed heroically to scare the predators away from her injured friend, while the sound coming from Fanta was half scream, half growl.

"Grab the other side of this, and we'll pull it out enough to give them room to escape."

They tugged, and space opened up, but instead of making a run for it, Fanta's screams got louder. Which was when Swirl realized her foot was still stuck. But the men must have figured it out too, because there was some yelling before the edge of the barrel lifted and Fanta shot out of there so fast Swirl could barely keep up.

They raced like the wind until they made it all the way back to the feeding station where Fanta stopped, and sat panting, holding her foot off the ground. The pretty white fur was tinged red with blood, but at least none dripped from it. Thank goodness, because blood would attract predators.

Carefully, Fanta worked on cleaning it up, but Swirl was certain she'd not be able to walk on it. Or climb to the safety of the trees. She sat beside her friend, determined to watch over her, but trying to think of a way to take her to a safe place like the big hay barn a whole day's walk away.

She'll need the ladies to help her.

Oh, Quark, thank heavens you're here. What should I do?

You must make sure the ladies see she's injured. They'll take her away and fix her up.

But maybe she'll be better tomorrow.

She'll be worse tomorrow, Swirl, and every day here in the forest will bring her closer to a painful death. It's your job as her friend to make sure she gets help.

Swirl hated knowing Fanta would have to go away,

but would do as she was told. She sighed, knowing how lonely it would be without her friend.

When the ladies came later, there was a kind of excitement in the air, and after the bigger cats had eaten their fill, and it was time for Swirl and the other youngsters to eat, the food wasn't put in the usual places. Instead, it was set inside the metal cages.

Swirl had eaten inside one of them before, but never such scrumptious-smelling food as this. Her tummy danced in anticipation. But just before she stepped inside, she looked back over her shoulder at her friend.

Fanta was trying to keep up, but it was hard for her to only use three legs and get over the branches and things on the ground. Quark's words echoed in Swirl's head. It was her duty to help her friend. The ladies were watching from far away, and Swirl guessed they brought the special food for her injured friend.

When Fanta finally caught up, Swirl rubbed against her in encouragement, then led the way to the food in the dish at the far end of the cage, where again she waited for her friend.

Once the injured kitten began to eat, Swirl dug in as well, a purr rising unbidden in her throat. Such tasty food it was, and there was plenty of it.

Her belly was nearly full when it happened.

SNAP!

Startled by the sharp noise and the vibration around her, Swirl's eyes grew even larger when she realized the opening she'd come in through was gone!

They were stuck once again, but this time was much different.

"It's okay, girls, we're here to help you."

The ladies came toward them, and there was nowhere to hide. Then everything went dark. Better. Dark was safer.

A sliver of light filtered in, and there was a face. Some clicking noises.

"I can't believe we were lucky enough to catch her. I

was really afraid she'd go into hiding."

"It will be good to have a buddy for her. Make her more comfortable in the feral recovery room."

"And two more uteruses off the street."

"I bet these girls will opt for life with humans. Did you notice neither has even hissed yet?"

"Shut down, likely. And maybe out of voice. The property owner said they both screamed blue murder when it happened. His poor workers felt terrible about accidently hurting her."

"Well they made up for it by letting us know she'd need our help."

Terrified, but hanging on to Quark's promise that everything would be okay as long as she looked after her friend, Swirl snuggled up against Fanta. Poor thing was panting so hard Swirl could almost feel the throbbing of her poor toes.

There was a frightening sensation of movement as they were lifted off the ground, and Swirl just couldn't help herself. *Quark! Help!*

It's okay, little one. You just have to believe. The ladies have never been anything but kind to us.

But I don't want to go anywhere! Will you still be able to hear me? To help me?

No, little one, it is time for you to be brave. Give the ladies a chance, and know that if you're really truly unhappy, they'll bring you back here to the forest one day.

What will I do without you there to guide me? I'll feel so very alone.

Your new life will be too busy for missing anyone, and if something goes wrong, Bobbi will be there for you.

Bobbi. Do I know her?

No. She was on her way to the rainbow bridge when we met some time ago.

I'm here. This new voice was even softer than Quark's. *I have you both now, and I'll watch over you.*

Be happy, little one.

37

Right after Quark's farewell, there was a loud, slamming noise followed by the sound of an engine like the tractor, but not as loud.

Sadness mixed with the fear of the unknown, and Swirl's heart ached as she snuggled against Fanta and waited for what would happen next.

***

SHE wrinkled her nose at the strange smells, but she couldn't see anything for a while. Then the cover came off one end of the cage they were in, and Swirl suddenly felt very, very small. It helped a bit when one of the ladies peering at them crouched down.

"What a pretty pair."

"The calico is just company. The ginger has the injured foot. We call her Fanta. You ready?"

"Sure."

"I'll use a towel and try to bring them both out at once."

The cage was opened and something big came at them. Hissing as hard as she could, Swirl put herself between the danger and Fanta, but then the thing dropped over them and everything went dark.

"You're okay."

"Poor little things are terrified. We'll start with an X-ray and go from there."

Fanta was taken away while Swirl was cleaned up, vaccinated, her ears cleaned, and her claws trimmed. Best of all, they set a dish of gushy food in front of her, and she was allowed to eat until her tummy was ready to burst and she couldn't keep her eyes open.

"Let's get her tucked into the blankets. Make things all nice and warm for the other one when she's finished."

Swirl had no idea what they were saying, but quickly learned about soft blankets when they settled her into them inside a crate.

"Here's something special for you." A large thing that looked a bit like a cat was put in with her. It had stripes, and was warm, and felt a bit like her mama.

Swirl woke up to find Fanta beside her, with a huge purple thing covering her sore foot.

"You're home girls," said the kind voice, and the crate door swung open.

Where are we?

Swirl peeked out. *I don't know, but this isn't our forest.*

"This is the bathroom, and yours to explore. There's not a lot of room, but I've made you another little cave to hide in behind the toilet. You've got a litter box with low sides for Fanta to get in and out of with her pretty cast, plus there's lots of food and water." She added some more kibble to a bowl. "I have to go now, but I'll be back real soon." The door slid closed behind her.

Fanta?

What?

You okay?

I dunno. My foot doesn't hurt like it did before, but there's this thing stuck to it.

Did they hurt you?

Not very much.

Quark was right. You're going to get all fixed up.

Maybe they can take this thing off my leg for me.

Maybe. What's a litter box?

I dunno.

Swirl crept out of the comfy blankets and carefully approached. Peeked over the side.

Well, what is it?

She sniffed the air, then climbed over the edge and found herself standing in soft stuff that moved around. She pawed at it and there was a funny sound. *It's kinda like dirt, but different.*

Dirt like to pee in? Cause I've really gotta go. Fanta tried to walk, but the big thing on her leg got in her way, and she had to go sideways and drag it along with her. She peered in. This was going to have to do. She hiked the clumsy attachment over the edge and squatted in the dirt stuff. Tried to cover where she'd gone, but the lump on her leg made it impossible, so she dragged herself out and went to check on the food dish. She hadn't eaten much at the place they called a vet office, and she was pretty hungry now.

When the lady came back, the kittens were snuggled together in the blankets.

"Have you two even moved?" She glanced at the litter box and the dirt stuff Fanta had dragged out behind her and laughed. "I guess you have. That's good you've been in the box, and. I see you ate, too, which is even better."

She sat on the floor close to them. "I bet you've never heard of fairy tales, but they're people stories with wonderful happy endings. Our version here is called a furry tale and it's when kittens and cats have had a rough time, but in the end, they get fixed up and healthy, and then they go off to live with people of their very own, who will love them for their entire lives. It's also going to happen to you two, and I'm going to make sure you always get to stay together.

She ran a gentle finger over the top of Swirl's head, and it felt so good she didn't move like she should have, didn't try to get away, and then the fingertip started to rub her ear and she found herself leaning into it.

Fanta's eyes had grown wide. *What are you doing? It's itchy.*

"You like that, don't you? How about—" Swirl was suddenly lifted through the air and into the lady's lap. Before she had a chance to summon a mighty hiss, a blanket was put over her and everything went dark.

"The ear mites should be dead, or at least dying, from the stuff the vet put on you, but let's get them cleared out of there." The blanket was moved around, and something poked into Swirl's ear, followed by more of the good feeling while the lady dug around.

"Wow. Look at all the gunk." She dug and dug and dug, and then did the same to the other ear.

Swirl? Are you okay?

Oh, yeahhhhh. When the poking and digging stopped, there was that wonderful fingertip again, rubbing and scritching under Swirl's chin this time, and making her eyes close. She started to drift off to sleep while the lady's soft voice continued.

"Once you two are feeling better, and we have you fattened up and healthy, we'll find you the perfect furever home, one with people who will always love you and watch out for you, no matter what. They'll make sure you have lots of food, and soft places to sleep, and there will be toys and fun, too." She set Swirl back into the nest with Fanta, and they snuggled together in the big pillow of softness.

"No more barns or tractors or big, nasty grain bins to fall on you. No more parasites to kill you from the inside, and no more wondering if there will be another meal. The only time your tummy will ever be empty again is the morning before your spay. But I promise, as soon as you wake up from surgery, you'll never feel hunger again. How does that sound?"

Amazing, thought Swirl, truly amazing. This indeed was a furry-tale ending to a very bad day.

5

RAVEN

THE black kitten was born under an old shed, where his mama made a cozy nest in the soft dirt so his brothers and sisters had stayed warm and dry for weeks. But he didn't know how to get back there.

He and his two brothers ventured out because they were very hungry when Mama hadn't come home for a long time. They'd already eaten the tiny creatures she left for them to play with after milk bar, but then their bellies ached from emptiness.

They'd thought following familiar smells would be a smart thing to do, but found no mice. Well, he did get a glimpse of one, and ran after it, but it got away. And while he'd been on the chase, his brothers had become lost, and now he was alone, except for *the voice*.

When she first spoke to him, he scurried about looking for her, not believing she could be invisible as she said. Finally, Quark, as she called herself, had just been there, standing in front of him. A beautiful gray cat with a tiny bit of white on her regal face.

She told him to watch carefully, and then she simply faded away. Now he understood. She was a very special cat. Called herself a guardian. Said she only spoke to those needing her help, and rarely showed herself to anyone, but his sheer stubbornness, his refusal to believe, and to listen to her, had made it necessary.

After that, he followed her voice while she talked about always watching out for predators. She taught him to scoot from one spot of cover to the next, carefully surveying with his eyes, listening, testing the air for strange scent. And before long, he found himself at a place full of good-smelling things.

He crept close to one.

You forgot to look around first.

Oh, dear. He zipped back to the branches he'd been hiding under. She was very strict. Just like Mama. He darted a glance all around, then heaved a sigh and started creeping forward again, hoping he'd get to the thing before Quark scolded him again.

He touched it with his nose, and it moved a bit, but the smell was so good he couldn't be afraid.

It's called a dish. And it's where the food will be later.

Again, the later thing. *When is later?*

There was a soft laugh. *I don't know. You will just have to wait.*

My brothers didn't wait for me.

They did. For a very long time, but you couldn't find your way back to them, and just kept getting farther away, which is why I brought you here instead.

But shouldn't I go back to them, to where Mama knows to find us?

She won't be coming back, youngster. There was an accident, and she had to leave here and cross the rainbow bridge.

Being a smart kitten, he remembered what Quark told him earlier about how she'd gone there too, but still came back to help others. *Will Mama be able to talk to me like you do?*

No, youngster, she has crossed over to stay. Only a few of us are able to go back and forth, but your mother is happy where she is, even though she misses her kittens. She's not tired anymore from raising endless litters. She did a fine job providing for the many she gave birth to in her short life, and will have no worries in the happy rainbow forest on the other side. She'll finally be able to bask in the sun, or spend an entire day doing nothing more than napping, or visiting with her kittens and other family who went before her.

So my sisters, will they be there with her?

Yes, the ones born too sick to survive, and your brothers who struck out from the nest with you.

They're dead?

I'm afraid so, which is why I'm being very strict about watching out for coyotes. You, young man, are the sole survivor of your litter, and there's a reason you were chosen. Therefore, you must always remember to be smart, and strong, and become a good member of the happy forest ferals, because these who surround you are your family now.

I don't see anyone.

Quark laughed. *You will, youngster, once your eyes adjust to what you're looking for. In the meantime, use your other senses, and you'll soon hear their breathing, smell their presence. You must fine-tune your receptors to the point where you know at all times where each of the others is located.*

He couldn't imagine such an ability, but wasn't about to argue while his tummy was rumbling with emptiness. While he listened to Quark tell him more rules about what to do when the eating began, he followed his nose from dish to dish, finding nothing in them to eat, but licking at the exquisite taste lingering on the edges.

He sat, and stared at the last shiny container. *I am awfully hungry, Quark, how do I find something to eat—*

Caw! Caw!

The horrible sound shot through him, and he was suddenly surrounded by rapid movement. He crouched low. Made himself almost as invisible as his guardian while cats of all shapes and sizes sprinted past him, every one headed in the same direction. Was a coyote chasing them? Did he dare to look over his shoulder to see?

No. Instead, he mustered his courage, leapt toward

the nearest tree and scrambled up until he could perch on a branch and look down at where the predator must be.

Nothing. He opened his senses as he'd been taught, and picked up only the excitement of many, many, cats now gathered far from the clearing. And then he saw something really scary.

A huge creature. It *had* to be a predator, of course, and it was walking on just two legs!

He stared, awestruck when he realized the other cats didn't seem to be afraid. In fact, some were following the predator, and others walking in front of it. And then things got even more interesting, because the creature went to the good-smelling dishes and filled them with stuff. The scent wafted up to the kitten and he nearly leapt from the tree.

The creature had to be what Quark called a lady. Said there were several of them, and they brought food every single day.

He struggled to remember everything the guardian told him about this place. There was just so much. Oh, right. He was supposed to wait until the others were finished eating before he approached, but he was very, very hungry.

Determined to get closer for when it was his turn, he gripped the trunk with his sharp little claws and started to let himself down a tiny bit at a time. But when he was only about halfway, his legs began to shake, and he couldn't seem to keep his grip.

Ohmygoodness. He was suddenly sliding, descending at a much faster pace than he'd intended, and he landed with a plop on the soft ground at the base of the tree…right beside the lady.

In the minute it took him to get his bearings, the tall predator nearly captured him, but he scooted away and hid behind an enormous orange cat who was eating at a wide dish. One wide enough for two, so the bold kitten tiptoed over to take a bite, but the low, warning growl had him backing away to hunker down and wait.

He glanced around at the other cats. Some were eating, and others were like him, waiting. There was a brown and black striped tabby also waiting behind the big ginger. She was watching Raven, but the expression in her eyes didn't seem to be threatening. She took a step closer, then another. Sniffed at him. He held his ground and tried not to hold his breath.

The tabby sat back to stare at him. *Hello, I'm Mila. What's your name?*

I don't have a name.

Where's your mama?

Something familiar about her voice made him eager to tell his story. *She went away, across a bridge, and I'm the last kitten left. We used to live under a shed, and I had brothers and sisters for a while. My mama was the same color as you, but with an orange stripe on her face.*

You're my sister's son. We searched for you after—

She said nothing for a minute, then sighed. *I don't have kittens of my own anymore, so I will take care of you. Watch over you for her, and teach you the ways of our colony.*

*But I already have—*he stopped. Didn't know if he was supposed to mention Quark.

A guardian angel? Yes, we love our queen. But now I'll lighten her load by taking you on and helping you make your way until...

Until?

Until you and the ladies decide about your future.

The ladies?

They'll take you with them one day when they leave, and after, it will be your choice if you come back here or move on to a different kind of life. But for now, you'll need to mind the order of things to stay out of trouble. The owner of the rump you're nearly leaning on is not always a friendly sort, so you might want to back up a bit and not crowd him.

The kitten did as he was told, but hated to be farther from the food again. *I'm very hungry. I haven't eaten since my mama left us.*

Then you will eat with me. Just be patient, and we'll get a turn soon.

He lowered to lie in the dirt, and tucked his toes under his chest. Everything was going to be okay. He believed what Quark told him. And now he had Mila, too. It still made him sad to know he'd never see his mama or his littermates again, but he wouldn't let himself think about it. At least not until his tummy stopped hurting so much.

The lady kept up a steady chatter to the cats around her while filling the dishes over and over again. Dozens ate, then moved away to carefully wash their faces while others took their turns.

When the ginger in front of him left the dish, Raven shot a glance at Mila, but she stayed where she was, apparently waiting for the food to be replenished. Then another ginger stepped up and took over the spot. *But…*

It will be our turn next, young man. You must be patient.

He hadn't known about patience when he was at the milk-bar, nor when Mama brought them mice to eat. But he was learning it now in a most unpleasant way.

This is called pecking order. Anyone new to the colony, as you are, is last in line, unless they have someone willing to share their spot. That's what I'll be doing, so you won't be the last to eat. But I'm way down in the order, which means you must still wait.

It is very hard.

And you're doing well. Occupy yourself with watching the lady. See how the other cats, at least some of them, play with the toys, and let the lady pet them? Some say it feels very good. I only remember being terrified when it happened to me. But maybe one day—now I'm home and feel safe again—I'll let a lady touch me.

Home again? Where were you?

The ladies took me away from here, and I had to live in a box the size of this clearing, with many scary smells and frightening noises. I didn't like being there, and every night, I sang the song of my people, hoping someone would find Sisko and me and rescue us from the prison.

Did they? Is that how you got to be home again?

No. It was the ladies. They said I could come home because I was so unhappy. It was a trying time. Especially with Sisko delivering an entire army of kittens. I wanted to help out, because she was as miserable as I was, but she was determined to look after them herself. I was glad when she was also allowed to return to the forest.

Did she get to bring her kittens?

No, they have a different kind of life now. They have people as their family, like the ladies. And they are always warm and safe and well fed. It's what every mother wants for her babies. None of mine ever had that chance.

The black kitten watched the lady make yet another round to refill dishes with the juicy stuff that smelled very good, and then there was a rattling noise as big containers were filled with kernels of something that also smelled delicious.

"Just in case you have any brothers or sisters lurking out there, young man. And I think I'll call you Raven, since you're black, and you fell out of a tree," said the lady as she placed one of the containers at the far edge of the clearing.

Was she talking to him? She certainly hadn't been looking his way.

"Are you watching over Raven, Mila? What a wonderful girl you are. I'm going to keep my distance until he gets a good bellyful of food. Just let me fill this up for you."

She scraped the contents of a big can into the dish the other cat finally vacated. "There you go," the lady said, and turned her back to walk away.

When he stood up to go to the bowl, Mila told him he must wait until she'd taken her position. Only then would he be allowed to join her. She walked toward the dish, veeerrryyyy slowly, then sat, curled her tail around to cover her toes, and began eating. Raven gave up on control and rushed to join her, took a ravenous lunge into the food, and lost his balance, tipping face first into the wet, mushy stuff. He sneezed and lost half the food in his mouth.

While he took a second, more controlled bite, he shot a glance at the lady, because she was making funny sounds.

She's laughing at your silliness, Mila explained before the lady started talking again.

"You're a hungry one, aren't you? I bet I could slip in behind you and scoop you up while you eat. But I have nothing to put you in, and I suspect you'd scratch my arms raw." She walked away then, and Raven quickly forgot about her as he gobbled great mouthfuls. It tasted scrumptious.

When he could hold no more, and was starting to feel just a bit sick, he sat back to wash his face, and again heard the lady's voice.

She was holding something by her head. "Eight weeks, tops, I'd say. Coal black. and just a bit floofy. Looks like Mila has taken him under her wing, and I expect he'll be okay until tomorrow. Great, I'll meet you here, and we'll capture him. Here—" She held the thing out in the air toward him for a minute or two, then put it back beside her head.

"I'm dying to just throw my jacket over him and scoop him up. Yeah, I know, if it doesn't work, I'll have scared him, and then it could be days before we get close again. Yeah, for sure. See you in the morning."

She stared at him, so he quickly scooted to Mila's side. "You, my little cutie, better stay safe tonight and get lots of rest, because your new adventure begins tomorrow."

She gathered a bunch of things into bags, then looked over again. "Keep him safe, Mila. We're depending on you, sweet girl." And then she went away, and the forest was silent but for the continuing sounds of cats eating.

His eyes drooped, and he struggled to stay upright, but kept falling to one side, and barely managing to catch himself before he hit the ground.

Mila's laugh sounded so much like Mama's. *Time for a nap, young Raven. Come with me, and we'll find you a safe place.*

He followed, feeling odd with his belly so full and his eyelids so heavy, but finally she stopped and turned to look at him. *Just a bit farther.*

She jumped up on a log, and walked its length to where the roots stuck up into the air. She pointed at a hollow spot.

You crawl in there, and I'll stay right here while you sleep.

***

HE woke up to full darkness, and it took a few minutes to remember where he was, and that he had no mama. He quickly stuck his head out, and when he saw Mila was right where she'd promised to be, there was a happy little hum inside him.

Time to make a move, young Raven.

Will we get more food now?

The ladies only come once in the daytime, and never at night. This is when we hunt.

Oh, for mice?

Yes.

They're very fast and terribly hard to catch.

You've tried?

Oh, yes, and the mouse was there, but then gone, and I couldn't find it. Not like the ones Mama brought to us. Those were much slower, and never ran far.

Your mama was teaching you well, and would certainly have taken you away from the nest for lessons eventually, and that's what we'll be doing now. Come along, and remember to always be aware of your surroundings. Stay alert so a predator can't sneak up on you.

Before dawn crept in to bring light back to the forest, Raven not only learned a great deal from his mentor, but enjoyed a fine feast as well, and when two ladies came to fill the food dishes, he wasn't nearly as impatient as the day before. He was content to sit beside Mila and wait his turn, but this time the lady didn't fill the dish when the ginger cat finished his share. Instead, she picked it up and walked away, towards a place where things looked different. Those food dishes were inside something square, and going in was sort of like going under the shed where he was born.

Mila hesitated at the entrance, and as Raven learned the night before, when Mila stopped, he was not to walk past her. So he waited.

When his mentor made a funny noise sort of like a growl, he backed up a step. *What's wrong?*

She turned around and swiped a tongue across his face, washed his ears, then sat back.

It's time for you to go now.

Go where?

With the ladies.

He looked over to where they were sitting on a log on the far side of the clearing. They didn't look like they were going anywhere. *I don't understand.*

Mila sighed. *You don't need to understand. Just go and eat now. I'll wait here for you.*

But you're supposed to eat first.

She made a small laughing sound. *You've learned your lessons well.* Then she led the way to the dish, but when he started to eat she backed away, and he didn't follow.

SNAP!

He swung around fast, to run to safety, but his way was blocked.

Help! Mila!

Shhh. It's okay, young Raven.

The ladies approached and he hissed at them, then everything went dark.

Mila! Quark!

I'm here, youngster. Quark's voice was low, and he had to concentrate to hear her. *You're going to be fine. Your next adventure has just begun. There will be many things for you to learn, but you'll be safe where you're going, and if you hate it there, you'll be allowed to come back one day. But I think you'll be very happy living with the people.*

Mila spoke from close by. *Make your mama, and me, and*

Quark proud, young Raven. Show the world how important you are. We will always love you, but there is even more love where you are going, so be brave.

Raven huddled in the corner behind the food dish. He didn't feel brave at all. How could he, when he was so scared? There was a sudden crack of light through the darkness, and one of the human predators peered in at him, making him wish he was even smaller and could be hidden by the dish.

"It's okay, little guy. I know it doesn't feel like it right now, but this is the best day of your life."

He stared at the big eyes, inhaled the strange scent, and suddenly, somehow he knew everything was going to be all right. *I'm going to be okay, Mila.*

I know you are, little one. I know you are.

Had he known he had something called ringworm and would have to endure frequent baths and quarantine for many weeks, he'd have been less quick to agree that things would turn out well, but in the end, they did.

The ladies at the shelter were always kind, and his food dishes were never empty. There were long hours when he was alone, but the times when people called snugglers came to visit with him were the best.

They played games with strings and feathers, and they petted him, and let him fall asleep on their laps, and eventually the quarantine was over, and after a visit to the vet for an operation, he went to live at a home of his very own with another kitten from the shelter.

They played together, and with short humans called children. There were days when they chased imaginary foes up the curtains, and under the beds, and there were other days when they'd just cuddle together in a sun puddle on the floor. As promised, the food dishes were always full, and they never needed to watch out for predators.

And when they were really desperate for a feel of the outdoors where they came from? There was a place called a catio for them to romp in. Yes, life was very good.

6

SYLKIE, DAX, AND WINSTON

SISKO laughed at the pair of youngsters batting a pinecone between them as though they hadn't a care in the world. But she knew how savvy they were.

They'd been born in the wild to a feral mom who'd taught them well, showed them the best hunting grounds. Today, with their bellies full of mice, boredom brought them to the feeding station.

Sisco bet the ladies would love to capture these happy boys. The silver tabby leapt in the air as he took a swipe at the cone and sent it flying across the clearing.

His brother—all black but for a white nose—was on it before it stopped rolling, and tossed it into the air with glee.

Other cats watched them play. Some with interest, others without expression, as though not sure what the boys were doing.

The mama cats were too tired to be amused. All their energy went into more important things, like eating so they could provide for their kittens—either the ones in their bellies, or the ones in their nests. Or both.

Sylkie, mama of these two scamps, was watching them from where they couldn't see her. She'd obviously followed the pair to make sure they didn't get into trouble they couldn't get themselves out of.

Heavily pregnant, Sylkie had to know it was time to move on, but she was such a good mom, she'd never turn her back on her babies.

Sisko skirted around the clearing to sit beside her.

They're beautiful and strong. You've done well.

Sylkie sighed. *It's very hard to let them go. They have such promise, but I fear for them being alone.*

The new ones will need your attention soon, and between the summer weather and the food from the ladies, these boys will be okay.

I suppose. But look at those silly kittens. So engrossed in their game, they don't even know what's around them.

Ah, well, they're about to get a lesson. If the cone gets any closer to Danny, he'll teach them a thing or two about boundaries.

As though she'd predicted it, the silver youngster galloped after the toy, batting at it until it bumped into the big ginger cat's behind.

Danny jumped, spun, and hissed at the kitten who was so startled he hopped backwards, got tangled up in his own legs, fell over on his back, then jumped up and ran to the nearest tree. He'd climbed up about six feet before he stopped to look down and see if he was being chased.

Kitty laughter rumbled around the clearing.

I don't think you have to worry about his reflexes, Sylkie. Where'd the other one go?

Up the next tree over when his brother startled.

You've done a good job, Mama, but if you'd like, I'll keep an eye on these two while you take a nap. The ladies will be here soon, so rest and then eat. Afterward, you can introduce me to the boys so they know to look for me when it comes time for you to go to your nest.

Oh, Sisko, how wonderful. Thank you.

I have none of my own anymore, and it would be a pleasure to watch over yours.

Do you miss having kittens?

Sometimes, but I don't miss the worry, the constant search for food close to the nest, and the fear of predators or toms finding my babies.

You've always been incredibly brave...and just a bit scary.

Sisko laughed. *I've been called intense, or focused, before, but never scary. Besides, now I'm just chill.*

And kind. Thank you.

Kindness was something she'd learned while in captivity—the endless time she spent pining for her family. The days had been hard. The nights much worse. But Sisko *did* appreciate how the lady had cared for her and her kittens, even fought for the life of the little one who'd had no chance of surviving. The human had fed him, kept him warm, tried to keep his tiny heart beating. He'd known nothing but love.

Sisko never had a chance to mourn a kitten before. But in that safe place, where there was an endless supply of food, water, and kindness, she'd felt saddened by the passing of Toothless, and those who went before him. There had been so many. Too many to recall. She couldn't even begin to remember the number of litters she birthed, and had no idea where many of her kittens were now, or if they were alive, or if they were safe and happy.

The only ones she knew about for sure were the seven the lady kept. Promised she'd look out for. And every time the ladies saw Sisko now, they assured her the kittens were healthy and happy, living with people who loved them.

True enough, indoors wasn't a life she wanted for herself, but for her kittens? To always be safe and warm, with full tummies? It was everything a mother could hope for. And then some.

At Sylkie's low trill, the two boys scooted down their respective trees and over to where she was quick to tidy them up with a swipe of her tongue.

I have someone special for you boys to meet.

Sisko took a step closer, and both kittens dove behind their mother.

This is Sisko. She's your aunt.

A tiny, silver-striped face peeked out. *Hi.*

Hello, Dax.

How do you know my name?

Your mother told me.

Oh.

You reacted well to a threat a few minutes ago.

I wasn't very brave.

Being brave isn't always the best answer. Running away from danger is a very smart thing to do. Only a fool would have done otherwise, and you don't seem to be foolish. Your mama raised smart boys, and I know you'll be survivors in this forest life, and you'll grow big and strong if you keep your wits about you.

A small black face poked out from behind Dax.

Hi, I'm Winston. He edged closer. *You look like my mama, but smaller.*

I'm your mother's sister from a different litter.

He tipped his head sideways. *I don't understand.*

Your mother and I have the same mama, but I was born the summer before her.

Do you have kittens for us to play with?

No. The ladies fixed it so I can't have any more.

Ever?

Ever again. Sylkie, have you thought about it? Would you go with them if I was here to look after your boys?

Where are you going, Mama?

Nowhere yet. But maybe someday I'll go.

And never come back? Mama, no!

Her laugh was a bit shaky. *I'd come back here.*

You know they'll give you an option.

I know, and a second chance if I'm not ready. Like Sloane.

Quark and Bobbi say she's very happy now, living a life of leisure.

I'm happy for her. And I know I should go for the sake of the kittens I carry now, but I'm not brave like you, Sisko.

You don't need to be brave, and heaven knows I wasn't. I wanted to change my mind the moment I realized I was captured. But bravery isn't needed. All you need to do is be patient and tolerant.

It sounds doable, but…

Talk to the others who've come home in the last few months. There are even more safe nests now in the place where the ladies take you, just like where I had my kittens, where it was so warm and soft.

But I'll never see my babies again.

True, unless you decide to stay with the people as well, and then maybe you'd have the same home as one of them. But even if you come back here, your kittens will get homes with people who will care for them. They'll never have to struggle in any way. Sisko glanced at Dax and Winston. *Unlike with these two, you'd never have to worry about your last litter's safety.*

It sounds wonderful.

It is wonderful, Sylkie.

In a scary way, though.

True, but as a feral mom, you've been sacrificing your own needs since you were only six months old. Why not make this a grand finale? A big gesture. Spare your daughters the fate of birthing their own kittens before the year is over.

Caw! Caw!

They're here.

Sylkie backed away from Sisko. *I can't. It's too soon.* She scrambled for cover, trilling at the boys to follow into the underbrush at the edge of the clearing.

Sisko's sadness for her friend was tempered by knowing at least Sylkie was *considering* going with the ladies, and it was the next best thing to taking the leap.

She sat back and enjoyed the sound of kibble rattling into dishes, but, even better, the tops being popped off cans. Yum. She'd grown very fond of mushy food while in captivity. And toona. Nothing quite like the smell of toona wafting through the air.

No small wonder the ladies used it in the traps. Sylkie hadn't tasted toona yet.

Was it wrong to encourage Sylkie to leave her boys? Go away while they still might need her? If now wasn't the right time, when was? There would always be another litter to consider. How would Sylkie ever get to have a life of her own? And what better chance did the kittens she carried have than with the ladies? What if something happened to Dax and Winston while she was gone?

Don't doubt yourself, Sisko. The voice was the softest of soft, and sounded like music.

Quark! Thank you. When I see her with those two boys and how happy she is with them...

They are not her destiny, Sisko. Remember how tired she looks, how her belly sags with new life while her milk bar is still filled for her last kittens. She deserves better, and we owe it to her to make sure she gets the chance.

Sisko smiled inside. *You're right. Thanks for reminding me.*

You're one of mine too, which is why I was allowed to stay behind in the beginning, and why now I am free to cross back and forth. When we volunteer for the program, we're helping prove the worth of all ferals. It's about more than toona, my friend.

Sisko's laugh bubbled. *But the toona is magnificent.*

Further incentive for you to escort others into the traps.

I shouldn't need incentive.

You hated captivity. A little toona helps get past that part.

It helps, but your support, and getting to mentor sweeties like Sylkie is reward in itself. And looking after those scampy boys, will be a joy. She puzzled for a minute. *Do you think the ladies will want to take them from us?*

They'll want to keep them safe, just as we do, and we'll have to wait and see what happens.

Sylkie fretted just a bit while she kept her boys hidden in a place where they could observe how pecking order worked. She pointed out the cats first to eat, those who waited one back, and others who boldly skipped the queue, only to be reminded with a hiss or a growl that it wasn't their turn yet. A hard lesson after learning bold and pushy at the milk bar was the key to survival.

Mama.
Yes, Dax?
Who is that?
Where?

The black one over there. He has only one eye.

It's Rollins. He's a gentle soul. One likely to allow a hungry boy to eat with him. Something worth remembering, just in case.

Just in case? What does that mean?

It means one day you or someone else might need his kindness, so it's a good thing to remember. Maybe she *was* ready to make the bold move.

But we have you, Mama.

Her heart nearly broke. How could she consider leaving this sweetness behind? As though on cue, one of the kittens in her belly gave a hefty poke at her insides to remind her how much was at stake. The two healthy kittens she'd leave behind had a good chance for survival, but they were the only two left of the six she'd given birth to only eight weeks earlier. *Oh, my beautiful son, I have to go away for a while, and you need to learn how to watch out for yourself.*

Don't go, Mama.

She touched his nose with her own. *One day, very soon, I'll leave you with Sisko. She'll help you while I'm gone, and then, before you know it, I'll be back.*

He seemed content with that. Maybe this was the right time. But she'd rather her boys not be there when she was trapped, because she was afraid she'd get panicky, and they'd end up scared of the ladies and the traps. That would be wrong, because one day they'd need these ladies. Maybe sooner rather than later.

She glanced over to a place where she'd never eaten before. It was where the trap could fall down over her. She'd seen it happen to many others, and always avoided eating there, especially when the ladies were very quiet, and had the long strings everywhere.

Sisko came up beside her. *Would you like me to go with you?*

What do you mean? You've already been there and back.

I'll go under the trap with you, and we'll eat together.

But when it comes down?

They'll let me out, and I'll watch over your boys then.

Sylkie's gut clenched, and when a belly kitten kicked in protest, she nearly laughed. These babies wanted to live, and she needed to give them the best chance she could.

They're nearly ready to be born, Sylkie, and you'll be busy with them, so busy, before you know it, you'll be back here.

Sylkie watched Mila move over to where the two kittens were hovering behind Rollins. *Hello, Dax. Hello, Winston. I'm another auntie like Sisko, and this is Rollins. He's one of your uncles.*

Come on, Sylkie. Sisko rubbed against her. *They're occupied over there. Let's go get some toona.*

Sylkie didn't let herself think about what she was doing. She just walked alongside Sisko and started to wolf down the food as if it was her last meal. Whoosh, thump! She closed her eyes and stayed frozen in place while her heart beat double time.

You're good, Sylkie. It's going to be okay.

I'm terrified!

Of course you are. You're a feral cat.

She heard the footsteps and her heart pounded even harder.

Open your eyes, Sylkie.

She blinked. It was dark.

There's a blanket over the cage, but this is the hard part now. They're going to let me out, and then put you in a smaller cage. I promise they won't hurt you.

Sisko prepared to launch when the opening came. *You're smart and brave, and we're proud of you, Sylkie.* And suddenly she was gone.

Everything else that day was a curious muddle of impressions. And all she could really remember was first Quark, congratulating her on her bravery, and then the sweet voices of her boys saying they loved her and would behave while she was gone.

The next real, solid memory was of the place she lived now. It was small compared to the forest, but there was a soft, warm nest for her kittens, and food, and water, a place to go to the bathroom, and ferns smelling like home.

And on the heels of those observations, came the first twinges of labor. She'd known how close she was, and wasn't surprised it was time, although apparently the ladies were a bit startled by the quiet arrival of the first kitten.

He was a scrawny tabby with a big voice, and by the time she had him half cleaned up, he was already latched on. The other four came quickly, and she struggled to keep up with her duties. The kittens and the nest needed to be kept completely clean and free of scents that might attract a predator.

When she was finally able to rest, she slept deeply, although for only a short time, and when she woke, the lady came in and brought her a dish full of food, just like Sisko said she would.

Kittens kept her busy for long days and nights, and there were times when the lady came and stole them away, which was terribly disconcerting, but for the most part it wasn't a bad experience, and the kittens were doing well.

And for the first time Sylkie's entire litter was still alive when it came time for them to start prowling around the nest.

Five sets of tiny eyes peered at her every time she returned from eating, and Sylkie's heart swelled with pride when she saw how healthy they were.

So far, Sisko was right about everything. She grew to know when the door would open, and even stopped worrying when the lady took the kittens away for short periods of time. She always brought them back, told Sylkie what a good job she was doing, and then left her alone.

And then one day she smelled something familiar. There was toona in her dish, and she knew it was time to return to the forest. She was sleepy after she ate, and her memories of being in the carrier were fuzzy. There were many strange and frightening noises and smells, and then after a long time in the carrier, she was back in her beloved forest.

When the crate door opened, she shot out of there so fast, she nearly careened into a tree before she stopped and took a good look around. Got her bearings and called out. *Sisko!*

Mama!

Her heart swelled. *Dax! Winston!*

The boys scooted out from under some brush and ran to her side. Sisko followed, but stood back and waited.

Sylkie immediately went to rub against her friend. *Thank you for encouraging me to go. My kittens are alive and well, and these two scamps have grown big and strong.*

They're smart boys, too. The ladies have been trying to trap them, but they keep evading. Sylkie glanced over at the two, who were already distracted by a white toy rat similar to the one the ladies gave her to play with where she'd gone to have her kittens.

Were you tempted to stay? asked Sisko.

No, I like the air here, and even if the beds aren't as soft, or the forest nearly as warm, it's my home, and I love it.

Sisko brushed against her. *Welcome home, my friend.*

***

A FEW weeks after Sylkie returned to the forest, Sisko spotted her watching Dax and Winston interact with the lady filling food dishes at the feeding station.

Perfect timing.

Sisko edged closer to her friend.

Your boys are like you, very brave.

Sylkie sighed. *I was terrified when I went into the trap, and while I was in captivity.*

That's what bravery is, Sylkie, doing what's right, even when you're afraid.

The ladies are going to take my boys soon, and I'll never see them again.

Sisko understood the sadness very well, because she

herself had known she'd never see the kittens she left behind when she refused to be socialized. *I try remembering that while I won't get to see them grow up, at least the kittens who stayed with the ladies will have good lives. They'll never have to worry about predators, finding shelter, or scrounging for their next meal.*

I know it's true. Even while I was there, I grew to understand what it felt like to fall asleep without worry, to eat whenever the mood struck me, and to not need to fret about anything.

You worry now about all those things, and about the futures of your boys.

I should encourage them to go into the traps.

I don't think you'll have to. They're enjoying playtime with the ladies so much, I think they'll make the move soon enough.

You're right, of course, but if I tell them about what to expect ahead of time, so they know, as I did, it will be easier for them.

Exactly.

Sylkie stood and stretched. *I'd best do it now, before it's too late.*

She uttered the low trill that called her boys to leave the toy they were playing with and scurry to her side. The pair were belly low when they reached her.

What is it, Mama?

What's wrong?

Nothing's wrong, my boys. But I need to talk to you about something very important.

When the two sat facing her—they were months old now, no longer tiny, but wide-eyed and serious—her heart melted, and she nearly changed her mind. How could she give up such incredible kittens?

Because she loved them enough to do what was right for them, even if it broke her own heart. Wouldn't the pain be tenfold if she ever had to watch them suffer? See them cold and hungry, or injured? Killed?

She took a deep breath.

You boys have taken a shine to the ladies who bring the food and play with you, which is a good thing.

They're very kind.

I like their soft voices.

That's good, it bodes well for your future.

Dax ducked his head. *I liked when one touched me the other day.*

Winston stared at his brother. *When?*

When we were chasing the string, and I was right by her hand, and she just touched me.

Winston's eyes widened. *What did it feel like?*

Nice. Sort of like when Mama brushes against me.

Sylkie knew for sure then. It was time. *Do you remember when I went in the trap?*

Yes. You went away for a while, and Aunt Sisko watched over us until you got back.

That's right. I went with the ladies, and they were kind to me.

Did they touch you, too?

Yes, and it did feel good. She stared off into the woods for a moment, thinking. Besides saying what her youngsters needed to hear, she was telling the truth. Even though she was afraid, and they'd wrapped her in a blanket and forced medicine into her mouth, she liked the way the fingers scratching under her chin made her feel safe somehow.

She'd even caught herself leaning into ear rubs, and once nearly purred before she caught herself. The memory was a good one.

The ladies are very good, and kind.

I know, Mama. They bring food every day.

And they play with us, too.

Yes. She swallowed hard. It was time.

Boys, the ladies want to give you a chance to have a life with people like them. To live in houses.

But we live here in the forest with you.

What is houses?

Do you remember the barn?

Both heads nodded.

A house is like the barn, but people live inside, and they like to have cats live there with them.

Sylkie continued repeating what she was told while wrapped in a blanket in the lady's lap one day. She'd been trying to convince Sylkie to stay and have a life with humans. But she had her boys to come back to. And now they were waiting for her to continue, as though she was telling a bedtime story.

The ladies want you to go with them, to see if you'd like that kind of life.

Will you be coming with us, Mama?

She fought the lump in her throat. *You're getting to be big boys now, and soon you'll be off on your own, not even thinking about me.*

And by then the few tomcats who'd avoided the traps so far would be chasing the boys away the minute they showed any interest in the females. There would be fights, and sometimes wounds became infected, and young males died, or were blinded, or lost use of a limb.

The ladies will set up the traps one day very soon, with dishes of very special food inside, and you'll both go in, because it's the smart thing to do.

Winston looked worried. *What if I don't want to go away?*

You'll be brave, and you'll make me proud, because you'll go anyway. Just to try the other kind of life. You'll stay there unless you are absolutely certain you don't want to live indoors, and then if you're sure, the ladies will bring you back here.

Will you be disappointed, Mama? Will you be sorry to see me return?

She lowered her head to brush her son's worried brow with her own. *I love my boys. If you decide to come back to the forest, either of you, I'll welcome you no matter what, I'll respect your decisions and I'll always love you. On that you can depend.*

But still we must go.

I want you to have the chance to make a good decision. One based on experience.

Dax tipped his head sideways. *Will we get to meet our cousins, Aunt Sisko's kittens who live with humans?*

I don't know, but I suppose it could be possible.

Rain began to patter on the leaves and brush surrounding them, and Winston squirmed while Sylkie licked some drops off his head.

Be still, son. And he was, so she indulged herself by giving his face and ears a good wash. Maybe—no *probably*—for the last time. She could see the ladies setting a trap close to where she and her boys usually ate. Her heart stuttered. This was it.

She took her time finishing Winston's wash, then did the same with Dax.

By the time she was done, the smell of toona was wafting through the clearing. She glanced over and met the steady gaze of the lady who'd cared for her when she went into the trap weeks earlier.

"You know I'll take good care of them, Mama," she said, as though reading Sylkie's mind.

So it would definitely be today.

"Whenever you're ready, Mama. It will be easier for them if you go in, too, and I promise I'll let you out if you don't want to come with them. It's your choice."

Sylkie had already decided to take them into the trap herself, and was steeling herself against the fear she knew would come the moment the door sprung. But she needed to be with them. Her last selfless act as a mother.

Winston, Dax, it's time for your new adventure.

Adventure?

What fun! Where are we going?

We're going into the trap over there, and we'll have some toona together. Then I'm going to leave you there, and the ladies will take you to a wonderful place where you'll play with toys and learn lots of fun things.

You're not coming with us?

No. I have to stay here to help Sisko and the others who watch over the kittens needing extra attention. To help them find adventures like the one you're going on.

What is toona?

Something magical and very, very tasty. Come along.

Sylkie's heart pounded against her ribs as she started across the clearing with her sons in tow.

She stopped at the entrance to glance over at the lady where she was partially hidden behind a tree.

"You're a good mama, Sylkie."

She took a deep breath and stepped inside. Hesitated for only a second, then made her way to the back where a dish filled with toona beckoned.

Winston and Dax followed to sit alongside her, and they ate together for a minute, before she gave them each a swipe with her tongue.

There's going to be a big noise now. Brace yourselves.
SNAP!

Mama! Dax scooted to get even closer to her, and she rubbed her face against his. *The scary part is over now, so your adventure can begin. Go back and eat some more.*

She gave Winston an affectionate rub too. *Eat up. It's a special meal today. Sometime I hope you'll think back on this moment and remember how much I love you both, my sons. Be good, be well, and one day, many years from now, I'll see you again.*

She left them at the dish and went to the end where the door had snapped shut.

The lady came then, laid a blanket gently over the cage, and when she crouched to look inside, tears were streaming down her face.

"I'll never forget what you did, Sylkie. You're the best mama, ever." She opened the door, and Sylkie slipped back into the forest that was her home. Rain splattered on the leaves, and she shook drips from her ears.

Maybe one day she'd be ready to go and live with humans, too, but for now, she'd join Sisko, who was waiting for her in the shelter of a fallen tree.

She walked straight to her friend, leaned against her, brow to brow. *My heart hurts. But not as much as I thought it would, because I'm happy my boys will never suffer the wrath of a mean tom, or an unforgiving winter.* Three of their lives had already been used up just in surviving birth, and the first few months of life as a feral. Their two sisters hadn't been as lucky.

Sylkie curled up beside Sisko and closed her eyes. Dreamed of her kittens romping together, perhaps with those small beings called children, in a safe place with soft cushions and dishes filled with delicious food. A furry-tale ending for sure.

7

TANADOR

HE'S back.

Quark's announcement spread throughout the colony. Even those further afield, and those who rarely showed their faces at the feeding station, crept closer to witness the homecoming.

Tanador been gone for a very long time, so long most had assumed he would never come back—that he'd died, or joined the ranks of the formerly-feral by choosing to live with the humans.

But Quark knew he'd return.

Tanador's struggle to survive after the accident was epic, and he was down to just one life now, having used up three in as many months. The first of those when the car hit him.

His scream still echoed in Quark's head. A dreadful memory—so like her own last day as a forest feral, when she foolishly crossed the road without looking. But her end had been swift and irrevocable.

Quark shook herself free of her personal ending. Went back instead to the day everyone raced to Tanador's side. So dreadfully still. Barely breathing.

Oh, Tan. Delilah's voice shook as she rushed to lie

beside him to keep him warm.

Wolfe gently licked his face. *We're here with you. We won't leave you alone, brother.*

Hurts so much. His voice was a mere gasp. *Can't move.*

Quark watched over them all, and her decision was not made lightly.

Tanador, you still have four lives left. And I'll not allow you to waste them here on cold pavement.

It would be hours until the ladies arrived to feed and few other cars passed this way. This was the time to call on a special angel who, like her, had permission to cross back and forth at will.

Bobbi? Are you near?

Yes, Quark.

Good. That's good. Tanador won't survive without the help of the ladies. We need you to get one of them to come right now. He desperately needs help, Bobbi.

I'll see that he gets it, my friend.

Bobbi's only physical ability was to move air, which could be a problem for some, but she knew her targets well. And luckily both women were at the rescue center just then.

She sent a breath across the back of one neck, then the other, stirring up the fine hairs, and was pleased when both ladies rubbed at the disturbance. One shivered, got up, and looked out the window.

"It's beautiful today. Why do I suddenly feel chilled?"

The other lady frowned. "I feel it too." She abruptly straightened in her chair. "Something's off." She scooted down the hallway to check on the two mama cats in residence, but found them napping comfortably.

"Everything's fine here," she said when she came back. She rubbed at her neck again. "Home?"

Both grabbed their phones and made quick calls but found nothing wrong at home.

"My neck's still tingling. What about the colony?"

As though reading each other's minds, they grabbed

their things and hurried out.

Quark? They're on their way.

Excellent, Bobbi. I knew I could count on you.

It was nice to be close to my people. I'll stay on this side in case you need me again.

Thank you, my friend.

***

WHEN the ladies arrived, Delilah and Wolfe stayed put.

"It's Tanador." One lady dropped to her knees beside them. "He's alive."

You need to let them help him now.

Wolfe and Delilah backed away, but kept watch.

"We can't put him in a crate. Hang on." One ran to the back of the car and pulled out an old cupboard door and an armful of towels and blankets, while the other talked into a square thing.

"He's not moving at all. Respiration is rapid. Pupils are big and round. No visible wounds. Yep. Okay. See you in ten."

She stuffed the square thing back in her pocket and touched Tan's forehead with gentle fingertips. "We're going to pick you up, and it's probably going to hurt like the dickens, but you have to hang in there, big guy."

They each slipped their hands under him, then carefully set him on the blanket they'd put on the piece of wood. With another light blanket overtop to keep him secure, they carried him to the back seat, where one strapped in beside him, and the other went around to the driver's side, then glanced back at Tan's two solemn friends still sitting at the side of the road. "You guys did a great job looking out for him. I promise we'll work just as hard to save him." Then she jumped into the car and pulled away slowly.

Quark made one of her rare appearances then, and

head-bumped both Wolfe and Delilah. *You did a wonderful thing for Tanador, and it won't be forgotten.*

Will he ever come back?

He'll be gone for a very long time. But he's destined to return someday.

We'll be here for him when he does.

***

TANADOR was too critical for immediate surgery, but he surprised the vet and everyone else by surviving the night—in spite of two close calls, when he stopped breathing for almost a full minute. But by the next morning, he was stable and they not only got his bones set and all four legs casted, but he was neutered as well, and his prognosis was upgraded to guarded.

Guarded, mostly because no one knew what to expect from a feral cat. Would he tolerate captivity, the casts, and the forced immobility? Would he eat and allow his caregivers to help him with bathroom duties while he couldn't stand or even sit up on his own?

All questions were answered within the first forty-eight hours.

He'd given himself over to the humans. Completely. Ate what was put in front of him, drank water, and rarely tried to move. Tanador was something of a limp rag in many ways, because there was absolutely no fight or resistance in him—for the first month.

But when the casts were changed, he changed. He no longer waited for help with the litter box, but instead he'd drag himself there to do his best—which was messy, to say the least—then growl the whole time the team member on duty cleaned him up.

And after the casts were removed at the beginning of his third month in captivity, he stayed out of reach as much as possible when humans came to tend to him, each day. Becoming more and more like the feral he'd been before the accident. He was once again the sly tom able to avoid neutering by never once stepping inside one of the traps.

One sunny day when he was stretched out on the windowsill enjoying the warm, and wishing he could be outdoors, the ladies arrived.

"This is your big day, Tan. You're finally going to get your wish."

"Hard to believe we're taking him back after all this time. I really expected him to turn in his feral card. Decide he wanted to live the easy life."

"Yeah, me too. But we have to respect his decision, and there's nothing more he needs from us. He's whistle-clean, inside and out. No worms, no ear mites, and no more gingivitis."

"His coat isn't as luxurious as when he was living outdoors, but it's coming back slowly." After the accident, much of it fell out, and some grew back white. But that was changing again, and his fur had a healthy shine to it now.

Tanador maintained his position on the window ledge, carefully eating the treats set there for him, but staying out of reach of the hand doing the delivery.

"Time for some tuna." She popped the top off the can, dropped the contents into a bowl and set it inside the crate where they'd been feeding him for weeks now, in preparation for today.

Tanador used the shelves mounted on the wall to make his way down from the high ledge, and walked into the crate for his meal.

The door was quickly closed, and the big cat didn't lift his head until the crate was hefted into the car. He'd been back and forth to the vet enough times that another ride was like old news…until the car door opened and he caught a whiff of familiar air. Home!

He leaped to his feet. Pawed at the gate and yowled.

The lady laughed. "Yeah, you were meant to come

back here."

The other door slammed. "We're not turning you loose on the road, and we expect you to never, ever cross it again, okay? You must have used up more than a few lives surviving the last trip, so no more, okay?"

"You think he'd actually try it?"

"Hard to say. But I hope not." She glanced around. "Weird there aren't any cats here to meet us."

"We're way early today."

"Yeah, but still."

Tan interrupted them, yowling more loudly.

"Okay, okay. Just hang on a sec."

They carried the crate across the road and into the forest…and there they were. Dozens of cats positioned along the pathway, solemnly watching. Then they fell into line, following all the way to the feeding station.

When the crate was set on the ground, Wolfe and Delilah were right there to stare in.

Delilah trilled, and rubbed against the screen. *You came home, just like Quark said you would.*

Bro. Wolfe was a cat of few words.

The crate door was suddenly open, and Tanador didn't waste any time thinking about his exit. He bounded out, went about three long strides away, then stopped to stare back at the ladies and the cage. Continued to stare for a minute, then with Wolfe on one side and Delilah on the other, he marched over to the marker where Quark was buried and rubbed his face against the wooden cross.

Quark.

Tanador.

I survived because of you.

No, Tan. You survived because of me, and Wolfe, and Delilah, Bobbi, the ladies, the vets, the techs. If any one element had been missing, the outcome would have been different. Every role, big and small, played a part in the whole.

He understood that. *I'm blessed to belong to this wonderful family.*

That you are. There are many not so fortunate, but because of us, and the ladies, more people are learning that all lives matter.

Even a stinky old tomcat half dead on the road?

Even him.

Quark brushed foreheads with the three cats perched in her sunbeam, then headed across the rainbow bridge to nap on her favorite fluffy bed. The one that made her think of happy clouds in a bright blue sky.

Tears poured down the cheeks of the ladies while they watched Tan curl up where the sun shone on the graves of those who hadn't survived their run-ins with cars. Delilah and Wolfe snuggled up alongside him, and dozens of others joined them in the tiny graveyard to celebrate the lives saved, and honor those lost.

Preview

CATS, Volume 2

1
MISTY, CLOUD, AND FOG

Misty, a kitten barely twelve weeks old, left her brothers partially hidden by a bush while she stalked a fat pigeon pecking at grain between railroad ties.

An empty belly her only concern, Misty was out in the open and the lessons her mama drilled into her were little more than a whisper in the back of her mind.

Hunger gave her tunnel vision, and she was bellied down like a seasoned hunter, prepared to take a creature almost double her size. Her heart pounded as though too big for her insides, and her toes vibrated with the need to spring.

She crept a bit closer, locked onto her target, and shifting weight back and forth in preparation for takeoff, her butt wiggled. One breath in, one out, another in—and she soared through the air, stretching her front legs out as far as they would go, and spreading her tiny claws.

Just when they should have sunk into shiny gray feathers, something rammed into her, scraped down her back, and knocked her to the ground.

Run! someone shouted. And without a thought, she burst free of the mass of feathers and raced for the low bush where her brothers were huddled.

Eyes wide, Misty goggled at the enormous hawk standing on the tracks, right where she'd gathered to leap.

The urge to turn and flee deeper into the forest warred with her conscience. She had her brothers to think of. They weren't very brave, and she promised her mama she'd watch out for them. Should she make a run for it so the hawk wouldn't see the boys? *Oh, Mama, help us!*

You're doing fine, Misty. That surely wasn't her mama's voice. No, in fact, it sounded like the one shouting at her to run a minute ago.

Who? She darted a glance around, but couldn't find the speaker.

I'm Sailor.

Where…?

Want to know more about Misty's adventure?
CATS, Volume 2, is available now in print and ebook.
Links at kathrynjane.com

ABOUT THE AUTHOR

Rescuing cats has been a lifelong endeavor for Kathryn Jane. It began at the age of five, when a neighbor told her he would have to drown the kittens she'd been playing with if nobody wanted them. She promptly gathered them up and took them home, but her father and the family dog said no dice and they had to be returned.

At seven, having learned the hard way, when Kat found a stray kitten in the warehouse behind where she lived, she left her there, but made a soft bed and took food to her every day. But alas, the dog and dad intervened again, but this time at least, a good home was found with her cousins and the kitten grew old with a wonderful family to care for her.

At sixteen, again, Kat smuggled a kitten into the house, but this time, she got to keep it, and has never been without at least one cat in her home since.

When Kathryn began writing mystery and romance novels, it wasn't surprising when a cat or two spiced up the adventures, and it seemed only natural that after watching TinyKittens ferals online, new ideas for stories were born.

Born also was the desire to help, which is why *all profits from the print version of the first book, CATS, Volume #1* will go to the TinyKittens Society of BC, Canada.

13186981R00051

Printed in Great Britain
by Amazon